George Washington Carver

by Vicky Franchino

Compass Point Early Biographies

Content Adviser: Professor Sherry L. Field,
Department of Social Science Education, College of Education,
The University of Georgia

Reading Adviser: Dr. Linda D. Labbo,
Department of Reading Education, College of Education,
The University of Georgia

 COMPASS POINT BOOKS

Minneapolis, Minnesota

Compass Point Books
3722 West 50th Street, #115
Minneapolis, MN 55410

Visit Compass Point Books on the Internet at *www.compasspointbooks.com* or e-mail your request to *custserv@compasspointbooks.com*

Photographs ©: Stock Montage, cover; George Washington Carver National Monument, cover (background), 4, 6, 7 (top and bottom), 16, 17, 26; George W. Carver Exhibit, Ottawa County Historical Museum, Minneapolis, Kansas, 8; Tuskegee University Archives, 9, 18, 21, 25; Simpson College Archive, Indianola, Iowa, 10, 11, 24; Iowa State University Library/Special Collections Department, 12, 14; HultonGetty/Archive Photos, 13, 15; E. R. Degginger/Bruce Coleman, Inc., 19; Bettmann/Corbis, 22, 23.

Editors: E. Russell Primm, Emily J. Dolbear, and Laura Driscoll
Photo Researcher: Svetlana Zhurkina
Photo Selector: Julie Barth
Designer: Bradfordesign, Inc.

Library of Congress Cataloging-in-Publication Data

Franchino, Vicky.
   George Washington Carver / by Vicky Franchino.
      p. cm. — (Compass Point early biographies)
   Includes bibliographical references and index.
   Summary: Simple text describes the life and accomplishments of the African American scientist who promoted the idea of crop rotation and found many uses for peanuts.
   ISBN 0-7565-0112-1 hardcover : libraperm paper)
   1. Carver, George Washington, 1864?–1943—Juvenile literature. 2. African-American agriculturists—Biography—Juvenile literature. 3. Agriculturists—United States—Biography—Juvenile literature. [1. Carver, George Washington, 1864?–1943. 2. Agriculturists. 3. African Americans—Biography.] I. Title. II. Series.
   S417.C3 F73 2002
   630'.92—dc21   2001001576

Table of Contents

A Great Scientist

George Washington Carver was a hardworking man. He became a famous scientist.

Life was not easy for George. His family was poor. George's mother was a slave.

George was African-American. He had to deal with **racism** against African-Americans. George never gave up hope. He never stopped working to help others.

◄ George Washington Carver

Growing Up

George Washington Carver was born around 1864. He was born a slave on a farm near Diamond Grove, Missouri.

George as a boy

A couple named Moses and Susan Carver owned George's mother, Mary. When George was born, the United States was fighting the American Civil War (1861–1865). This was a war between the Northern and Southern states.

During the war, there was a lot of crime in Missouri. One day, people who stole slaves **kidnapped** George and his mother.

Moses Carver

Moses Carver paid a man to search for them. Only George was found. His mother was not. So Moses and Susan Carver took care of George and his brother, Jim.

◄ George, far left, with his brother, Jim

A Love of Learning

George loved to learn. Susan Carver wanted George to go to school. But there was no school for black children in their town. Back then, black children and white children did not go to school together.

So when George was twelve, he left the farm. He walked 8 miles (13 kilometers) to go to a black school in Neosho, Missouri.

In Neosho, George met Andrew and Mariah Watkins. They let George live with them. George helped take care of their garden.

George attended many schools, including one in Minneapolis, Kansas.

Painting was one of George's hobbies.

George was happy in Neosho, but the school was not very good. George knew as much as the teacher!

In 1878, George moved to Fort Scott, Kansas, to find a better school. Then a terrible thing happened. George saw some white people kill a black man. This made George afraid. He decided to leave Fort Scott.

George moved from town to town and school to school. George liked to learn about plants. He also liked music and painting.

9

After High School

George Washington Carver
as a young man

George Washington Carver finished high school in 1885. He wanted to go on to **college** and learn more.

George wanted to go to Highland College in Kansas. But when the **principal** saw George, he said he could not go to school there. Why?

He couldn't go to that school because he was African-American.

George was hurt and sad. For a little while, he tried farming. It was a very hard life. In 1889, George sold his farm and moved to Iowa.

George applied to college again. This time he went to Simpson College in Indianola, Iowa. George studied painting. He was the only black student at the school, but he got along fine.

George Washington Carver visited Simpson College in 1941.

Iowa State University

Soon George decided he wanted to help poor black farmers. He wanted to study **agriculture**.

In 1891, he left Simpson College. He went to Iowa State College of Agriculture and Mechanic Arts. Today it is called Iowa State University.

At first George was not happy. He was not allowed to live or eat with the other students because he was African-American. But soon

George, second from right in the back row, with other students at Iowa State College

Booker T. Washington

things got better. George made friends and joined clubs.

George graduated from Iowa State in 1894. For two years, George stayed and worked there as a teacher.

Then he got a letter from a man named Booker T. Washington. Washington was the principal of a school for blacks in Alabama called the Tuskegee Institute.

Washington wanted George Washington Carver to come to Tuskegee. He wanted George to teach the students about farming. George agreed.

At the Tuskegee Institute

George was surprised by how poor Alabama was. He was surprised by how poor the Tuskegee Institute was too.

George felt that he had two jobs. He had to teach the students at Tuskegee. He also had to help the poor farmers who lived and worked nearby.

George, at top, far left, with other teachers at Tuskegee

Students working at Tuskegee

Most of George's students did not want to be farmers. They had grown up on poor farms and knew how hard that life could be. George decided to show them that farming could be a good life.

George taught his students about soil and plants. He showed them how to use **compost** to feed the soil and make it rich.

15

Cotton near Tuskegee was not very good because the farmers planted only cotton year after year. The soil was worn out.

So George taught the students to plant different crops. First the students planted peas. Then they planted soybeans. Then they planted cotton. The peas and the soybeans helped the soil. The cotton grew better than it ever had before!

George's work often took him out into the fields.

◄ George working in his lab

Helping the Farmers

The local farmers saw how well the cotton grew. They wanted George to help them too. George started classes for the farmers. But some of them could not read. Some lived too

A boll weevil ➤

far away to come to Tuskegee. So George put his school on a wagon and took it to the farmers!

Soon the farmers had good soil. They could grow fine cotton.

Then an insect called the **boll weevil** came to Alabama. It killed the cotton! What would the farmers do now?

◄ When the farmers couldn't come to school, George took school to the farmers.

A New Crop

The farmers asked George for help again. This time he told them to grow peanuts!

The farmers were not sure that was a good idea. At that time, only animals ate peanuts. But the farmers trusted George, so they grew peanuts.

The crop was very good. There was only one problem—no one wanted to buy the peanuts!

To help the farmers, George spent a lot of time studying peanuts. He found many new ways to use them.

Then George invited some people to dinner.

He served soup, chicken, bread, salad, candy, cake, and ice cream. All the food was made with peanuts!

The people realized that peanuts could help Alabama. If peanuts became popular, Alabama farmers would make money.

George had to find new uses for peanuts so that farmers would grow them.

In 1919, the farmers started a new group. It was called the United Peanut Association of America.

21

A Trip to Washington

The group sent George Washington Carver to Washington, D.C., in 1921. They wanted him to talk to **Congress** about their problems.

The group wanted to pass a law to help the peanut farmers. The law would make peanuts from other countries cost more than peanuts grown in America. Then people would buy

more American peanuts.

Members of Con-gress gave George only ten minutes to speak. They thought that talking about peanuts was a waste of

Edsel and Henry Ford with George

time. George surprised them. They listened to him and, in the end, they passed the law.

The newspapers printed stories about George. Suddenly, everyone knew who he was! Thomas Edison and Henry Ford, two famous inventors, wanted George to work for them.

◄ President Franklin D. Roosevelt met George Washington Carver at the Tuskegee Institute.

George said no. He wanted to be a teacher. He thought helping other people to learn was the most important job in the world.

George with a stack of fan mail

A Lifetime of Helping Others

George worked hard for the rest of his life. He found almost 300 ways to use peanuts! He discovered more than 150 ways to use sweet potatoes too. He taught farmers how to grow and use soybeans and pecans.

George never married. His students

George Washington Carver in his later years

GEORGE WASHINGTON CARVER

were his family. George gave his life savings to the Tuskegee Institute. He wanted his work to go on even after he died.

George Washington Carver died in 1943. He was almost eighty years old. Today he is remembered as a great teacher, inventor, and scientist.

George often had to deal with racism in his life. He believed that God put him on Earth to help others. George Washington Carver spent his life doing just that.

◄ George Washington Carver spent his life helping others.

Important Dates in George Washington Carver's Life

1864	Born near Diamond Grove, Missouri
1877	Leaves home for school in Neosho, Missouri
1885	Applies to Highland College and is turned down
1890	Attends Simpson College
1891	Moves to Iowa State College of Agriculture and Mechanic Arts
1894	Graduates from Iowa State
1896	Becomes a teacher at the Tuskegee Institute
1915	Booker T. Washington dies
1919	United Peanut Association of America is founded
1921	Speaks to Congress about peanuts
1943	Dies on January 5

Glossary

agriculture—farming

boll weevil—a harmful beetle

college—a place to continue learning after high school

compost—a mixture of dead and rotted plants that is added to soil to make it richer

Congress—a group of elected officials in the U.S. government

kidnapped—taken away forcefully

principal—the head of a school

racism—a belief that one race is better than others

Did You Know?

- In 1938, a Hollywood film was made about George Washington Carver's life.

- If George Washington Carver had not been a scientist, he might have been an artist. In 1893, one of his paintings won a prize at the World's Columbian Exposition in Chicago.

- George wore a fresh flower in his buttonhole every day.

- In the United States, January 5 is George Washington Carver Day.

Want to Know More?

At the Library

Coil, Suzanne M. *George Washington Carver*. New York: Franklin Watts, 1990.

Nicholson, Lois P. *George Washington Carver: Botanist and Ecologist*. New York: Chelsea Juniors, 1994.

Rogers, Teresa. *George Washington Carver: Nature's Trailblazer*. Frederick, Md.: Twenty-First Century Books/Henry Holt, 1992.

On the Web

e-Library at Iowa State University: George Washington Carver
http://www.lib.iastate.edu/spcl/gwc/home.html
For interesting information about George Washington Carver

National Inventors Hall of Fame: George Washington Carver
http://www.invent.org/book/book-text/23.html
For an audio file about George Washington Carver

Through the Mail

The George Washington Carver National Monument
5646 Carver Road
Diamond, MO 64840-8314
To borrow videos about Carver's life from the free loan video library

On the Road

Tuskegee Institute National Historic Site
P.O. Drawer 10
Tuskegee Institute, AL 36087
334/727-3200
To see the original Tuskegee Institute and the George Washington Carver Museum

Index

About the Author

Vicky Franchino has wanted to be a writer ever since she was a young girl and spent hours writing copy for fictional catalogs. As a freelance writer, she has worked for such varied groups as educational toy companies, greeting-card companies, and universities. She holds a bachelor's degree from the University of Wisconsin in Madison. Vicky Franchino lives with her husband and their three daughters in Wisconsin.